KETTLEBELL

The Ultimate Kettlebell Workout to Lose Weight

(Lose the Fat and Get Fit With Kettlebells)

Hazel Brady

Published by Tomas Edwards

© **Hazel Brady**

All Rights Reserved

*Kettlebell: The Ultimate Kettlebell Workout to Lose Weight
(Lose the Fat and Get Fit With Kettlebells)*

ISBN 978-1-990268-59-5

All rights reserved. No part of this guide may be reproduced in any form without permission in writing from the publisher except in the case of brief quotations embodied in critical articles or reviews.

Legal & Disclaimer

The information contained in this book is not designed to replace or take the place of any form of medicine or professional medical advice. The information in this book has been provided for educational and entertainment purposes only.

The information contained in this book has been compiled from sources deemed reliable, and it is accurate to the best of the Author's knowledge; however, the Author cannot guarantee its accuracy and validity and cannot be held liable for any errors or omissions. Changes are periodically made to this book. You must consult your doctor or get professional medical advice before using any of the suggested remedies, techniques, or information in this book.

Upon using the information contained in this book, you agree to hold harmless the Author from and against any damages, costs, and expenses, including any legal fees potentially resulting from the application of any of the information provided by this guide. This disclaimer applies to any damages or injury caused by the use and application, whether directly or indirectly, of any advice or information presented, whether for breach of contract, tort, negligence, personal injury, criminal intent, or under any other cause of action.

You agree to accept all risks of using the information presented inside this book. You need to consult a professional medical practitioner in order to ensure you are both able and healthy enough to participate in this program.

Table of Contents

INTRODUCTION 1

CHAPTER 1: CHOOSING THE RIGHT KETTLEBELL 2

CHAPTER 2: KETTLEBELLS – AN OVERVIEW 7

CHAPTER 3: THE HISTORY OF KETTLEBELLS: A FAD OR A LONG-LIVED FITNESS TOOL 25

CHAPTER 4: BEGINNER EXERCISES 35

CHAPTER 5: WHAT YOU NEED – KETTLEBELL 101 41

CHAPTER 6: KETTLEBELL FOUNDATION 52

CHAPTER 7: HOW DOES A KETTLEBELL HELP YOU LOSE WEIGHT? 58

CHAPTER 8: HOW HEAVY IS THE KETTLEBELL? 70

CHAPTER 9: BACK LEGS AND GLUTES 91

CHAPTER 10: REMEDIES TO COMMON MISTAKES DURING KETTLEBELL EXERCISES 99

CHAPTER 11: WORKOUTS 103

CHAPTER 12: KETTLEBELL ULTIMATE WORKOUTS FOR MEN 110

CONCLUSION 114

Introduction

This book covers all the factors that affect weight loss including workouts, resting and diet. By using the tips suggested in this book, you will be able to lose weight fast without the need for expensive equipment. The kettlebell exercises are really easy and they could also be integrated to the workouts that you are already doing. The nutrition principle suggested by this book follows the Paleo and low carb diet. We hope that you will reach your workout goals by using the tips suggested in this book.

Thanks again for purchasing this book, I hope you enjoy it!

Chapter 1: Choosing The Right Kettlebell

Depending on your desired results you will generally need more than one kettlebell. As if a kettlebell is the correct weight for your swings it will probably be too heavy for overhead presses or high rep snatchs. At a minimum I would recommend two kettlebells: one for pressing and high rep cardio workouts and another for lower-body work, such as swings, squats and cleans. For pressing men (beginners) start with a 16kg kettlebell while woman (beginners) start with an 8kg kettlebell. If you have good base fitness then a heavier kettlebell may be more suitable. 24kg is the Russian army standard for men and is a good multi-purpose kettlebell. For woman it would be around the 12kg weight.

For the lower-body lifts such as the deadlift a 32kg kettlebell is the starting point for beginning male and females a 16kg kettlebell. Once you become confident working with one kettlebell you can progress to working with two and take your training to the next level.

As for selecting the actual kettlebell in my experience there are three types; the cheap plastic covered kettlebells which I would avoid at all costs, the next are the cast iron kettlebells which are simple and functional. These are fine to start off with granted you are not doing high reps in which case many of these kettlebells handles are unsuitable and will tear up your hand. Proper competition steel bells are the ideal choice, as they all have the same dimensions regardless of weight. A 16kg kettlebell is exactly the same size as a 40kg kettlebell (except the 40kg is solid while the 16kg is nearly hollow.) This is done so that a competitor does not have to deal with different movement patterns only the change in weight. The handle is smooth steel so is kinder on your hand with high reps.

A Guide to Repetitions and Sets

As a general guide when working with reps and sets they fall into one of four categories; strength, power, hypertrophy and conditioning. If pure strength is the aim then 3-5reps and 3 sets should be your basic template. Heavy clean and presses as an example should be completed with strict form maintaining the muscles under maximum tension throughout the movement and lowered slowly. Weight should be 80%-100% 1RM (1 rep max.) Rest should be increased to 3 minutes between sets.

For targeting power a few more reps (5-7) should be undertaken and sets kept at 3 to 4. Weight should be reduced to 70% to 90% 1RM.

If hypertrophy is your aim (Body building to create large muscles.) Then sets and reps will be increased (10reps x 10 sets) at 60-70% 1RM.

If conditioning is your aim then a mix of cardio and strength through timed intervals should be your starting point. Using kettlebell swings as an example; use a stop watch and time 2minute intervals to see how many repetitions can be achieved. This can be increased by 1minute increments as fitness improves working up to one 10minute set when you are at competition level!

Using timed intervals works well for swings and snatchs were high repetitions are the aim while other exercises need a more structured rep range. Note that weight will need to be decreased if high repetitions are the aim.

Ladders are yet another option to mix up workouts, using clean and presses as an example; 5 clean and presses, then 4, then 3, then 2, then 1 before resting and starting the next set. Ladders can be especially effective when used in conjunction with timed intervals i.e. 3minutes of work, 1minute of rest, then 2minutes of work, 1minute of rest, and then 1minute to finish.

For a more brutal workout regime Tabata can be implemented, which uses 20 seconds of ultra-intense exercise followed by 10 seconds of rest, repeated continuously for 4 minutes (8 cycles). Ensure you have the correct technique of the exercise down before attempting this.

Throughout the book I have indicated an example of repetitions and sets which could be followed next to each exercise as a starting point but feel free to experiment with timed intervals if you feel the your workout needs a shake-up.

Chapter 2: Kettlebells – An Overview

WHAT IS A KETTLEBELL?

If you imagine a cannonball with a handle attached at the top, that is exactly what a kettlebell looks like. They are typically made from either cast iron or cast steel and their origins can be traced back to the Russian girya. The origins of the girya stem from the 18th century where it was used to weigh crops. By the 19th century, similar weights were being used by circus strong men as a display of strength. During the late 19th century kettlebells broke onto the scene of competitive and recreational strength athletics. In 1885 girevoy sport was born, a form of kettlebell lifting for competition. By the early 20th century kettlebells had gained worldwide recognition and the English name 'kettle bell' was coined.

BALLISTIC TRAINING

Kettlebells have gained popularity in the mainstream market for their versatility and efficacy as a full-body workout tool. The exercises done with kettlebells are called ballistic exercises or power exercises. To understand ballistic training more fully, you need to understand the formula for power.

Force x Velocity = Power

Or, to put it more simply: Strength x Speed = Power

Speaking of velocity, we are referring to both the speed at which a load, such as a kettlebell, is traveling as well as the direction it is traveling in. The force exerted can be equated to how much strength you are using to move and, more importantly, accelerate the kettlebell.

Strength and speed counteract each other in this relationship. The heavier something is, the slower it will move but more strength is required to move it. The lighter it is, the faster it will move but the less strength is required to move it. Therefore, it is impossible to train for both maximum speed and strength at the same time. The optimal training for the best results is to train in the middle of the two, at about 30% – 80% of your personal one-rep max in weight.

A one-rep max is the absolute maximum weight you can lift in a single repetition of an exercise, such as a bench press or a dead lift. If you can lift a maximum of 100 pounds, your ideal mid-point will be a kettlebell of 30 – 80 pounds for ballistic training. By having speed and strength meet in the middle, you are training more effectively and efficiently. You're moving as much weight as you can as quickly as you can without either strength or speed suffering by being too slow and heavy or too light and fast.

BENEFITS OF BALLISTIC TRAINING WITH KETTLEBELLS

Fat-Burning Power: Running has long been touted as the best exercise to burn fat and get lean. Kettlebells have kicked that misconception right out the window. The American Council on Exercise (ACE) performed a study that demonstrated that per one minute of swinging a kettlebell, you can burn up to 20 calories (No author. 2019, September 1). That equates to a 400 calorie burn in a 20-minute period. To burn 400 calories within 20 minutes of running, you would have to be running at a pace of six minutes per mile.

The After Burn: The high intensity of kettlebell workouts produces high excess post-exercise oxygen consumption (EPEOC). Simply put, it increases your post-workout calorie burn which amplifies the efficacy of the workout. The higher the rate of calorie burn and the longer the effect lingers, the more fat you will burn after your workout.

Long-Term Calorie Burn: Exercising with kettlebells increases your lean muscle mass. Muscle burns more calories than fat just to keep functioning; the more muscle you have, the more calories you burn at any given time, even while resting.

Ditch the Gym: You don't have to put off getting fit because you don't want to go to the gym. You can get strong, fit, and lean without ever leaving the house; all you need is a kettlebell.

Save Money and Space: Compared to other home gym equipment kettlebells are relatively inexpensive in the long term. You don't have to start out with a whole set of varying sizes, all you need is one kettlebell at the right weight for you and you're ready to get started.

Strong, Lean, Mean-Machine: Kettlebells will help you build muscle, but don't be intimidated. You are not going to lose your femininity to large, manly muscles. Working with kettlebells builds lean muscle. It will give you that toned, sculpted body you've always wanted, and increase your strength without the bulk.

Cardio and Strength: Kettlebell exercises combine the cardiovascular benefits of fast-paced movements with the strength training of using weights. You are targeting two different training goals with one workout, making it more effective and efficient.

Functional Strength: Training with kettlebells develops what is known as functional strength. By utilizing multiple groups of muscles in your body, your workout is building strength used to perform everyday activities, making you stronger and lowering the risk of injury.

Five-in-One Workout: Training with kettlebells doesn't just increase strength and speed. You will also improve your endurance, flexibility, and balance.

All-in-One Training: Forget about doing lots of different exercises that focus on single body parts at a time. Your training sessions will target multiple muscle groups at the same time, delivering a full-body workout in one session.

Right to the Core: Kettlebells are extremely effective at developing your core strength. Your core muscles stabilize and support your body. A strong core is essential to good posture, easy movement, and to prevent injury from performing everyday tasks.

Coordination: Training with kettlebells often involves a variety of movements and helps develop an awareness of your body. The connection between your mind and muscles and your focus will improve, leading to overall better coordination.

Alternative Cardio: You are combining speed and strength training, making kettlebell exercises an effective replacement for traditional cardio-based workouts. If you are looking for a way to ditch the treadmill, but still want to work on your cardiovascular health, metabolic rate, and burn fat, then kettlebells are just what you need.

Hip Power: The kettlebell swing is one of the most popular and effective kettlebell exercises. It helps train your hips for power and speed. Increased power in your hips leads to improved stability and a lower risk of injury.

Flexibility and Mobility: Kettlebell training is multi planar. You will be working on controlling the strength you are putting into the movement, the tongue, and the range of motion. Over time your limits will increase, giving you a wider and better range of motion and more flexibility.

Posture Perfect: Kettlebells strengthen your hamstrings, gluteal muscles, hip and pelvic muscles, lower and mid-back, trapezius muscles, shoulders, and neck. Simultaneously improving all of these muscles and your core develops good musculoskeletal support.

Get a Grip: Kettlebell training develops a firm, strong grip by working your wrists, fingers, and forearm. You can say goodbye to asking for help opening jars.

Evening the Playing Field: Most people have a dominant side of their body that is stronger than the other. Kettlebell exercises help you discover areas that need improvement and even out strength differences in your body.

Joint Health: Kettlebell workouts aid in improving joint strength, stability, mobility, and flexibility and ultimately increasing range of motion.

Keep it Simple: Kettlebells are simple. You don't need a variety of workout equipment, or to perform overly complicated exercises. Kettlebells are also highly portable, convenient for packing into your car so that you can work out whenever you have time, wherever you are. If there's one thing that will keep you on track with your exercise regime, it's not having an excuse not to work out.

ARE KETTLEBELLS FOR YOU?

Those who should give kettlebells a try include:

Any person wanting to reap the rewards that working with kettlebells offers

Anyone wanting to work out in the comfort and privacy of their own home

Any person who wants to change up their fitness plan or try a new workout plan that employs exercises that are proven to be effective

People suffering from back injuries who want to build muscle and train for strength, but do not want to put unnecessary or additional strain on their spine

Athletes who want to enhance their conditioning and overall performance in their chosen discipline

THE (VERY FEW) DOWNSIDES

As with everything else in life, kettlebells come with good points and a few drawbacks as well.

Expense: While they may not break the bank, good quality kettlebells still require a financial investment. The good news is that you can get started with just one and invest in more as you progress.

Form and Injury: The exercises and movements are dynamic, work on multiple planes, use large numbers of muscles at the same time, and require balance, stability, and strength. Correct form is essential to prevent injury, so it's important to learn and practice carefully and master form before strength.

Space: Kettlebells are small and compact compared to large home gym equipment, but they still take up space. You need to have a safe, out-of-the-way space to store your bells where you won't trip over them. You do not want to stub a toe against a cast-iron cannonball; trust me, it won't be fun!

Non-Adjustable: The majority of kettlebells are not adjustable. You will need to keep adding to your collection or replacing the kettlebells you no longer need with newer, heavier ones. Kettlebells are an ongoing expense over time to invest in your fitness, and not just a once-off initial cost. The bright side is that the cost isn't astronomical with each upgrade, and your fitness and body are worth investing in.

KETTLEBELLS VS DUMBBELLS: BATTLE ROYALE

Kettlebells and dumbbells have "battled" for popularity and preference over each other for decades. What is the difference and which one wins the title of top training tool?

Weight Loss

Winner: **Kettlebells**

Traditional dumbbell strength training may assist with weight loss but it's not very efficient at it and will take much longer than with kettlebells.

Bulk vs Lean

Winner: Kettlebells

Dumbbells isolate muscle groups and are often used to build bulk muscle. Kettlebells employ fluid movement, cardio, and strength training to build lean muscle for a sculpted and toned appearance.

Beginner-Friendly

Winner: Dumbbells

Dumbbell exercises are less complex and slower-paced for beginners to strength and weight training. Kettlebells will take some acclimatizing and practice to use with the correct form.

Incremental Increases

Winner: Dumbbells

Kettlebells come in fixed increments. This means that kettlebells are available in increments of 9 – 18 lbs. These are not small increments and can present a challenge when increasing the weight of your bell. Dumbbells offer increments of 1 – 2 lbs. at a time, offering the flexibility of increasing weight in smaller, more manageable increments.

Balance

Winner: Draw

When working with kettlebells, the weight is unbalanced compared to dumbbells. This may seem like a disadvantage but it's not necessarily a bad thing. With kettlebells, all of the weight rests at the bottom of a central handle, making them harder to wield. This is effective for improving balance, coordination, and working more muscles. Off-balance weights also offer different types of exercises and grip positions, making them more functional and versatile.

Dumbbells, on the other hand, offer more balance and stability. They are easier to use because of the better balance and require less coordination. This tussle comes to a draw because each is effective in a different way, dependent on what your goals are.

Grip

Winner: Kettlebells

The grip used for kettlebells and dumbbells is vastly different. Dumbbells offer only one style of grip while kettlebells offer a range of different grip options at varying angles. They aid in developing a much stronger grip than dumbbells because of this variation in grip and the unbalanced nature of the weight.

Handle Smoothness

Winner: Draw

The handles of kettlebells are smoother than the bars of dumbbells. Dumbbells need to offer the user a textured surface for a better, non-slip grip on them. Kettlebells need to have a smooth handle so that it moves freely and smoothly in your hands. Both handles serve their own purpose for the exercises they are intended for, so this battle ends in a draw.

Functional Strength

Winner: Kettlebells

Dumbbells target specific areas and muscle groups in limited, non-functional movements. Kettlebells employ a wider range of movements that target multiple muscle groups and emulate daily activities. This increases the functional strength used in your day-to-day life.

Cardio

Winner: Kettlebells

Dumbbells may leave you huffing and puffing from exertion when you're working with weights heavy enough to push your muscles to their limits. The downside is that for all this heavy breathing and sweating, it's not a cardio workout. Kettlebells employ exercises that provide you with a cardio workout and a strength training workout at the same time.

Mixing It Up

Winner: Kettlebells

Dumbbells are not as versatile and easy to just toss into an existing workout plan as kettlebells. If you are tired of your long-standing exercise routine, try adding some kettlebell exercises to shake things up a bit. Not only will it eliminate boredom, but you will also discover new muscles to work, build, and tone.

Time

Winner: Kettlebells

Dumbbells are tried and tested for strength training but that is where their functionality ends. Strength training with dumbbells requires a greater time input to work each isolated muscle group separately. You also then have to add cardio to your schedule. Kettlebells save you time by offering a dynamic, all-in-one full-body strength and cardio workout in one session.

Budget-Friendly

Winner: Dumbbells

Kettlebells may not be an expensive investment in your health and fitness, but they do still come at a cost. Dumbbells cut costs by making use of a single bar onto which you can stack interchangeable weight plates. The overall cost of dumbbells is generally somewhat lower than that of kettlebells but both are a good choice for home strength training and warrant the investment equally.

Chapter 3: The History Of Kettlebells: A Fad Or A Long-Lived Fitness Tool

You may have heard about kettlebells before. You may have even seen one at the gym or at a friend's house. Perhaps you saw one advertised, bought it immediately and now you're using it as a paperweight. That actually seems like a beneficial use for it. You may have actually used a kettlebell before. You may have used it on a regular basis and are familiar with it. Whatever your personal experience with kettlebells is, I am confident you will learn so much more throughout these various chapters.

The kettlebell has made a huge surge in the fitness world over the past couple of decades, which makes people think that it's something new and fresh. Many people think it's a fad like so many other things out there. Sooner or later, it will go away and be forgotten. Well, all I can say is, if it is a fad, it is the longest-running one I have ever known about. The kettlebell has actually been around since the 1700s, and maybe even earlier, making it one of the oldest exercise tools to be around today. Of course, a few adjustments had to be made throughout the years and centuries.

While the history is a little unclear, it is believed that the kettlebell as we know today originated in Russia around the year 1700. It was not originally used for exercise, but by farmers to weigh grain and other goods that they would be selling. During this period, it is believed that farmers would toss these kettlebells around and compete in feats of strength with one another during their downtime. The farmers would often get bored on long days and use that time to compete with one another for the pure joy of it.

These kettlebells became known as giri, or girya, which literally translates to "handle bell." The word girya was introduced into the Russian dictionary in 1704. After a while, the giri began getting used in various farming festivals and competitions involving these tools would play a central role. The kettlebell is still used to measure productivity in Russia and other countries that were part of the Old Soviet Union.

The main thing that changed about the kettlebell is the size and shape throughout the various decades and centuries. The ones we have today are shaped cylindrically, like a ball, with a sturdy handle for gripping. They also come in various sizes, weights, colors, and materials.

There is still much debate on the exact origins of the kettlebell and there have been numerous cultures of the past that have used a version of this equipment that predates use in Russia. Some historians even speculate that kettlebell style weights were used by ancient Romans and Greeks. There will always be major holes in history; however, it is hard to deny the amount of influence Russia had in making this tool a worldwide phenomenon. Even though it did take several centuries. Furthermore, the specific tools that were used by the Ancient Greeks, Romans, and even in certain Asian cultures are not considered the precursors to what we have now. They are not as closely aligned to the modern-day kettlebell as the ones used in Russia.

Around the turn of the 19th century, people started seeing the kettlebell in a different manner. Vladislav Kraevsky, who is considered the father of weightlifting in Russia, first introduced the kettlebell as a strength and conditioning tool. Kraevsky was also a doctor and personal physician to the Russian Czar. He popularized kettlebell training in the Russian army, and it was eventually elevated to a national sport in 1948. This piece of exercise equipment was kept a secret in Russia for a couple of centuries.

The kettlebell has some potential history throughout various European countries too as it may have been used by many other physicians and active life proponents. Many German training manuals and diaries from the 18th and 19th centuries feature the kettlebell under different names. Friedrich Ludwig Jahn, who was a gymnast and physical educator from Germany, featured many kettlebell exercises in his system of gymnastics. In Germany, Jahn is known as "Turnsvater Jahn" which means "father of gymnastics." He pretty much created the system of gymnastics that is the hallmark of the programs being used for physical education programs in the United States today. There are early photographs of his disciples using the kettlebell in old photographs.

Furthermore, there are photographs of strongmen and strongwomen using versions of the kettlebell prior to the 1900s. This was well before Dr. Kraevsky popularized it in Russia. The point here is that Russia played a major role in making the kettlebell a worldwide phenomenon, but the kettlebell is not uniquely Russian.

It seems to have many roots at this point without any definitive origin.

The kettlebell had a lot of growth during the 1900s. During the early 1900s, many circus strongmen traveled to and settled in America, where they opened many gyms and began giving people in the United States their first taste of kettlebell training. For some reason, during the 1940s and 1950s, this piece of equipment disappeared from US gyms without a trace or explanation. There are many theories about why this happened, including wartime distrust of anything Russian related and rivalries between different fitness experts. It is also possible the equipment lost its craze and went away for a while.

The Craze certainly never went away in Russia. It was as popular as ever during the mid-1900s. Techniques like the swing and juggle were popular folk exercises during the 19th and 20th centuries in many farming communities. As we mentioned before, 1948 is when it officially became a national sport. This was the year that

Russia declined to compete in the Summer Olympics, and instead, chose to have strongman competitions in Moscow.

Numerous sports schools began popping up throughout the Soviet Union during the 1950s, 60s, and 70s. Kettlebell training became known as a working man's sport due to its affordability and minimum space requirements. The first official kettlebell commission was formed in 1981. The commission advocated for mandatory kettlebell training for all workers, believing it would result in improved health and productivity.

The first national kettlebell championship in Russia took place in 1985. Further advancement came in 1989 when a 10-minute time limit was placed for kettlebell lifting competitions. Competitors were tasked to complete as many reps as possible during this time period. After the kettlebell was featured for the first time in a highly renowned Western athletic magazine in 1998, it has taken off in popularity. In 2001, it gained popularity in the United States and quickly became a worldwide phenomenon. This was the year that they were first manufactured outside of Russia.

By 2002, the kettlebell had already been entered into Rolling Stones Magazine Hot List as the Hot Weight of the year. This was a very high-profile recognition for something that was once a farm tool. This diverse piece of equipment has continued to take off from this moment. It has been accepted as a necessary exercise tool by many fitness fanatics around the world, including yours truly. Which brings us to where we are today.

The main thing I am pointing out here is that the kettlebell is not new. It predates modern time by centuries and the fact that it has been used in so many different settings is a testament to its versatility as a workout tool. If you are worried about the kettlebell losing its popularity, I don't see it happening soon. This simple tool has been around so long and utilized by so many different cultures, that it's hard to deny its effectiveness. This will become more apparent once we start talking about it.

Kettlebell workouts are legitimate and have been used by people from all walks of life for centuries. They will continue to gain popularity in the future as more people become aware of them. I am a huge fan myself and can't wait to show you the amazing results you can achieve. I am confident that once you learn all that this apparatus entails, you will make it the central part of your workouts. There are numerous kettlebell styles. If you are wondering if a certain type of kettlebell is right for you, then read on to the next chapter.

Chapter 4: Beginner Exercises

Kettlebell dynamic workouts enable you to strengthen your muscles and build your endurance.

Two-handed kettlebell swing

Targets: hips, glutes, legs, shoulders and back

Stand straight with your feet apart. Hold the handle of the kettlebell with your palms facing down and make sure that your arms are extended in front of your body.

Slightly bend with your hips pushed back. Lower your body slightly but avoid going too low. In a fluid and explosive motion, swing the kettlebell while keeping the core engaged. The motion should come from the hips and not the arms. Repeat the swinging motion 12-15 times.

Alternating floor press

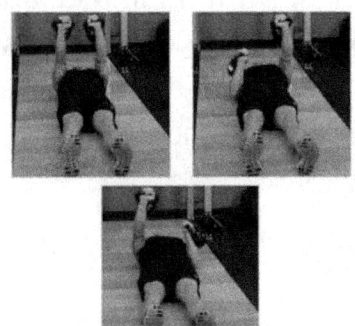

Targets: chest, shoulders, abdominals, triceps

Start the exercise by lying on the floor with two kettlebells on your side. Hold the kettlebells with your palms open. Extend your arms above your chest. Lower one kettlebell and bring it close to your chest. Turn your wrist in the direction of the other kettlebell. Raise the kettlebell and repeat on the other side.

Two arm kettle row targets

Targets: back, shoulders, arms

Take two kettlebells and place them in front of your feet. Bend slightly as you try to grab both kettlebells. Pull them towards your stomach keeping your elbows close to the body as much as possible. Lower the weights and repeat 12-15 more times.

Kettle pirate ships

Targets: shoulders, abdominals

Stand with your feet wide apart. Hold one kettlebell with both of your hands. Let it hang at waist level with your arms extended. Start your movement by turning into one side and swinging the kettlebell at head level. Take a brief pause when the kettlebell reaches the top. Drop the kettlebell and rotate to the other side. Raise the kettlebell again to the other side. Repeat the movement 12-15 times.

Goblet squat

Targets: Quadriceps, calves, hamstrings, shoulders and glutes

Hold a 5 pound kettlebell close to your chest. Stand with your feet apart. Squat low until your legs are on your hamstring.

Keep the kettlebell close to your chest. Make sure to keep your head up and your back straight. When you are in the bottom position, use your elbows to push your knees out. Stand up and return to the starting position. Repeat 12-20 times.

Extended range one arm kettlebell floor press

Targets: chest, triceps, shoulders

Start by lying on the floor and hold a kettlebell in one hand. Make sure that you grip tightly on the kettlebell handle. The leg on the same side as the kettlebell should be bent. Cross your knees over the midsection of your body. Extend the arm holding the kettlebell and press it above your body. Return to the starting position and repeat several times.

Chapter 5: What You Need – Kettlebell 101

Being successful with this program means starting with a quality set of kettlebells consisting of multiple different weights.

A **good kettlebell** will be made of metal, not plastic or vinyl. It should feel sturdy and stand up to being dropped or rusted. I prefer kettlebells to have a rough surface, but some will have a smooth, metallic surface. They won't hold chalk as well and may become slippery, but they will still be usable.

If you do not have a set of kettlebells for your garage or basement gym space, find a gym that has a set. Most gyms, even larger fitness centers, will have a set of kettlebells. I like to workout at home though, and I was able to build my collection over the course of a year to spread out the costs and have a great set of kettlebells for my workouts.

There is a difference too between training and competition bells. A training kettlebell will usually be a little more utilitarian looking and the sizes will vary as the weight increases. A completion bell will often have an outer coating that is colorized and the size will stay the same as the kettlebell weight increases.

In the past, kettlebells were measured in pood, which is a Russian weight system where 1 pood is equivalent to 16.38 kilograms or 36.11 pounds. Recently though, kettlebells are becoming standardized to kilograms and in some cases pounds. It is generally more acceptable to see them in kilograms.

The three parts that make up the kettlebell are, starting from the top, the handle, horns and bell.

The handle is where you grip the kettlebell. Some handles have a small circumference so they can be held easier while others will be thicker and can be more useful for grip training as a result. Some manufacturers will use a wide grip to allow for easier two-handed swinging while others will have a slightly more rounded handle shape and make it harder for a two-handed grip.

The horns are the part of that connect the handle to the bell. For some exercises, such as a goblet squat, you will grasp the kettlebell by the horns. The horns will generally be the same circumference as the handle, but shapes and angles can vary by manufacturer.

The bell is the heavy lower part of a kettlebell and it is where the majority of the weight it located. The offset nature of the weight is what makes the kettlebell so effective, and the bell is where most of this weight resides. I like a kettlebell with a flat bottom and flat side so that it tucks into my arms when I perform certain movements. Otherwise, a bell will usually be round and have the weight of the kettlebell.

While they look cool, I'd recommend avoiding kettlebells with designs on one side of the bell – sure, it looks cool to do a heavy clean with a monkey-face kettlebell, but it isn't entirely necessary for the cost and could interfere with movement.

Buy what you need

I'll often get asked what weights are best to buy. That's a hard question to answer without knowing the person specifically and what they are capable of athletically, but we can make some general prescriptions.

If you are a beginner lacking in strength and experience, start with smaller weights. A pair of 15, 25 and 45 might be a good progression to begin with. This will allow you to perform and learn the movements we will use in this book in a safe way. If you can find if for a cheap price, you may even want to buy a 10 pound kettlebell for practice reps.

If you have been using **kettlebells** for a while, then you can start with heavier weights. I'd recommend the following:

2 x 35lb

2 x 45lb

2 x 55 or 65lb

1 x 75 or 80lb

With this range, you will be able to do everything from lighter warm-up and skill work sets to heavy working sets.

The heaviest weight (75 or 80 lb) will be reserved for lower-rep kettlebell swings or goblet squats. It is important to get doubles of the lower weights for things like double clean, press, squat and snatch or farmers carries. Turkish get-up which generally use less weight, but as you get proficient in the movement you may start to experiment with higher weight for lower sets.

Other equipment

While this book focuses on the kettlebell, there are some other implements that will increase the effectiveness of workouts and add to strength, power and endurance. Before we move on, let's take a quick look at some of this equipment.

If you are a member of a gym, most of this equipment will be available for you. However, if you want to build a home gym, add this equipment to a budget and shop around for the best prices. You can visit my blog at **www.jvictorfitness.com** for links all of these implements.

Sandbag

A **sandbag** serves variety of functions and is an excellent way to build grip strength while doing traditional movements like rows, cleans, presses and shouldering. In this way, it can be a substitute for a barbell at a fraction of the cost. Moving a sandbag from the ground to one shoulder, or shouldering as it is called, is an often overlooked movement that has an amazing effect on strength and endurance.

You can make your own sandbag or purchase one. I have seen designs for homemade sandbags that use tire inner tubes, duffel bags or even just plastic bags and duct tape. I purchased a sandbag kit that has a strong, water resistant outer and handles and has smaller filler bags inside of the larger bag to help distribute the weight.

One of my absolute favorite exercises is to load up a heavy sandbag and walk. This long heavy carry will increase your heart rate and build leg and core strength.

Slam Ball

Think a basketball meets a sandbag and that's a **slam ball**. Slam balls allow you to perform unconventional weighted movements like the ball slam where you pull the ball from the ground to overhead then throw it back down - it's an excellent core movement and has a surprising effect on arm and upper-back strength and size. I love to use slam balls for weighted rucking too, either carrying it on my back or stomach and walking. Either way, slam balls add a lot of bang to your workouts and are a great way to fill in space in a conditioning circuit with unconventional movements.

Pull-up bar

The most basic yet most necessary of piece of gym equipment, **a pull-up bar** allows you to build strength throughout your entire upper body. Prioritizing pulling strength has direct implications for fitness.

We can put strength into two categories - absolute and relative. Absolute strength is your ability to move weight like with a barbell or stone. Relative strength is strength relative to body weight and is mainly used with bodyweight movements. So, for example, being able to do 30 pull-ups is a marker of relative strength whereas pulling a 500 pound deadlift is absolute strength. Pull-ups are an excellent way to build relative strength as they target shoulders, lats and core - three main areas of relative strength.

On a pull-up bar you can do: Pull-up, chin-up, bar hang, towel pull-up, mixed grip pull-up, muscle-up, bar crawl, knees to elbow, toes to bar, hanging leg raise, burpee to pull up.

Mace

A **mace** is another unconventional training implement that can add benefit to your training. Like the kettlebell, a mace has an offset weight which gives a different stimulus than a barbell or bodyweight movement. Simple movements like a mace squat or lunge can add some flavor to a training session and more advanced movements like the mace 360 can target muscles that normal exercise don't.

Sled, prowler

Pushing or pulling a heavy load simultaneously builds strength, power and endurance.

Generally, a **sled is an object you pull and a prowler** is a contraption you push. A prowler will have two uprights to hold and push on - maybe think about a football training session. Sleds will often be a small piece of metal with straps to grab and pull. I purchased a sled from Rogue Fitness that uses Olympic bumper plates for weight, but you can build a sled if you don't have access to a purpose-built alternative.

When you use a sled, consider using other grip options too. Instead of just pulling it with the sled behind you pull facing the sled to target your hamstrings, or pull with a rowing motion to bring in your back and hips.

Barbell and bumper plates.

The best way to build absolute strength and raw power is with a **barbell**. It's the reason why it is used in powerlifting, Olympic weightlifting, CrossFit and general strength development. Powerlifting movements like the deadlift, squat, press and Olympic movements like the clean, snatch and jerk are the go-to techniques for seeing massive increases in strength.

Unfortunately, a good barbell setup can be expensive to purchase, which is why the kettlebell is becoming so popular. However, if you have access to a barbell setup, consider taking a movement a week, like the deadlift or squat, and use a barbell for the sets.

Chapter 6: Kettlebell Foundation

They may not look like much, but kettlebells are an all in one gym. As you've probably noticed, kettlebells have a unique design that sets them apart from other training apparatus out there. A kettlebell is a cast iron weight that looks very much like a cannon ball, but with a handle attached. The thing that makes this equipment super effective is the design of the handle, which allows for the center of mass of the kettlebell to extend beyond your hand. This makes the kettlebell an ideal piece of equipment for such ballistic movements as swings. Ballistic movements are a great choice because they integrate cardio, strength and flexibility training all in one awesome movement.

Ballistic movements also allow you to develop functional fitness that copies activities that we perform in the real world, such as shoveling snow.

There are two prime functions of kettlebell training:

(1) Developing functional fitness

(2) Training specifically for kettlebell competition

In this book we will focus exclusively on functional fitness movements that will rid your body of fat while building muscle, leaning you up and boosting your fitness.

Getting To Know Your Kettlebell

Kettlebells can be either fixed load or adjustable. Obviously, fixed load kettlebells are quicker and easier to use, as there is no having to change resistances between movements.

The kettlebell handle is the part of the equipment that you will most frequently come in contact with. Kettlebell handles may vary from very smooth to very rough. You want one that is neither too smooth nor too rough, but will allow for a firm grip when your hands get sweaty.

The unique shape of the kettlebell makes it a superior choice for many exercises. The shape of the weight and the distance between the handle and the ball allow for swinging and catch and release movements. It also allows the weight to sit directly against the arm, providing for greater leverage. Providing for neutral alignment of the hand and arm also allows for greater endurance of the arm muscles throughout the exercise.

The kettlebell sets in your gym will typically range from 8kg (18 pounds) to 48kg (106 pounds). The average man should start with a 16 kg (35 pound) bell, while most women begin training with an 8kg (18 pound) bell.

Clothing Considerations

Try to avoid wearing loose fitting clothing that is liable to get caught up in the kettlebell during such movements as swings. You should also stay away from slick logos and designs on your clothing that are going to make you sweat a lot and make it increasingly difficult to keep your arms by your sides.

Don't wear pants that are too baggy. You don't want your thumb or forefinger to get caught up in the baggy part of the crotch when you are performing swing type moves. Tight fitting shorts are a great idea.

Safety

Ensure that there is a clear space of one square meter (3.3 square feet) around you when you are working with kettlebells.

If you get in trouble with a rep, don't try to save the rep – simply move out of the way and let gravity take over.

If you can, use chalk to prevent your hands from becoming too slippery.

Have a towel on hand to wipe off sweat.

Stay hydrated throughout the workout.

Wear wristbands to prevent chaffing of the wrists and forearms.

Wear shoes with hard, flat soles.

Always lift and lower the kettlebell under control (bend you lower back!)

Kettlebell Movement Technique

Most kettlebell exercises will involve one of two grips:

Finger hook grip

Hand insertion grip

A palm up grip begins by inserting your middle finger through the middle of the kettlebell. Place the index finger under the thumb to create a finger grip hook.

You should avoid the following common grip mistakes:

Gripping the handle too tight

Holding the handle too loosely

Holding only with the fingertips

Kettlebell Breathing Technique

There are two types of breathing used with kettlebell training; Paradoxical Breathing and Anatomical Breathing. When engaging in brief, heavy, high intensity training you should use paradoxical breathing. A set that lasts longer and uses a lighter weight should be accompanied by anatomical breathing.

Paradoxical Breathing

With this type of breathing you inhale during the eccentric part of the movement and exhale during the concentric part. As an example, with squats you would inhale on the way down and exhale on the way up.

Anatomical Breathing

Anatomical breathing is the reverse of paradoxical breathing – you inhale during the concentric part of the movement and exhale during the eccentric part. This type of breathing is ideal for endurance training.

Chapter 7: How Does A Kettlebell Help You Lose Weight?

Kettlebells are one of the simplest and most effective weight loss tools around. The weight of a kettlebell is centered below the handle, so it needs a lot of energy and muscle work to counteract the momentum. There are many reasons to why kettlebells are becoming the most popular choice of weight loss.

Burn More Calories in Less Time

Kettlebells are different from traditional free weights because traditional weights aim at certain muscle groups only and rest of the body muscles remain static. Kettlebell training is very demanding; it does not isolate muscle groups and gets your whole body moving. This results in much more oxygen and energy requirement and leads to burning of huge amounts of fat in a very short span of time.

Burn Calories Even After Training

Excessive post-exercise oxygen consumption (EPOC) or Afterburn refers to the loss of calories that occurs after training due to increased metabolic rate of the body. Kettlebells can produce an afterburn effect that may last for more than 24 hours.

During an extensive training session, the muscles' demand for oxygen increases creating an oxygen shortage, and causes the body to ask for more oxygen after training. More oxidation results in more fat breakdown which causes weight loss.

Kettlebell exercises are high-intensity exercises. High-intensity exercises result in lactic acid accumulation in muscles and depletion of body's oxygen stores. As a result, the body is forced to work harder in order to replenish the oxygen stores for a period of 24 to 36 hours post-training.

Which Kettlebell is Right for You?

Picking the right kettlebell is essential in order to get the most out of kettlebell training and to avoid injuries. The selection of a kettlebell depends on various factors such as type of training, age, gender, weight, fitness level, and previous experience with kettlebells.

Type of Training

There are many different types of kettlebell exercises; generally we can divide those kettlebell movements into two categories:

1. Ballistic Lifts

Ballistic lifts include kettlebell swings, snatches, judging, and tossing. Ballistic lifts usually require a heavier kettlebell but beginners should not put a lot of stress on themselves because strength building with kettlebells takes time; therefore, it is better to start with a lighter kettlebell and perform the exercises effectively before moving on to a heavier kettlebell.

2. Kettlebell Grinds

Grinding movements include get-ups, windmills, overhead presses, and bent press, which result in constant tension on the muscles and a greater chance of muscle injury. Grinding movements require attention to whole-body tension and regulation of sustained power breathing; therefore, these exercises are usually done with a smaller kettlebell.

Gender

Kettlebell choices for men and women are different because of the difference in their body strengths. Generally, it is seen that women tend to choose lighter kettlebells, whereas men over-estimate their strength and end up choosing a kettlebell too heavy to endure. Starting kettlebell weight for men and women is different and depends on their level of fitness and type of training.

Kettlebell Sizes for Men

Kettlebell training is technical and requires a lot of strength and experience. Therefore, choosing a kettlebell size that is reasonable to start with is important.

12 - 16 KG – Men with very little strength and small-build are advised to start with a

kettlebell of 12kg to 16kg. Individuals with medium-build who had recent rehabilitation from injuries or have low fitness level and experience with kettlebell can also start with similar weights.

16 - 20 KG: Kettlebells of 16-20kg are best suited for men of medium build with average strength and fitness level.

20 - 24 KG – Strong, athletic, active men with an extensive training experience and high fitness level can start with a kettlebell of 20-24kg.

The choice of kettlebell is also affected by the type of training. For ballistic movements, average-build active men should start with a 16kg or a 20kg kettlebell. Athletic men with medium to large build can start with a kettlebell of 16kg or 28kg.

For grinding movements, choose a kettlebell that you can easily press overhead about eight to ten times. Active men can start with an 8kg kettlebell, while athletic men can choose a kettlebell of 12kg.

Kettlebell Sizes for Women

For women, starting weight of kettlebell depends on their current level of fitness and exercises that they intend to perform with it.

8 - 12 KG – This is the ideal weight to start with for most women, especially for those who have small build, very little training experience, and who have undergone recent rehabilitation from injuries.

12 - 16 KG – Women with average build and little strength training experience can start kettlebell training with a 12kg or a 16kg kettlebell.

16 - 20 kg – Women who have an extensive strength training experience, very good cardiovascular fitness, and strong build can start with a 16kg or a 20kg kettlebell under the supervision of an experienced instructor.

For ballistic movements, inactive women should start with a 6kg or an 8kg kettlebell. An 8kg kettlebell is the most popular starting weight for women who are active but new to kettlebell training. Athletic women can start with a 12kg kettlebell also.

For grinding movements, inactive women should start with a 4kg kettlebell. An average, active woman can start with a kettlebell of 8kg and athletic women can start with a 12kg kettlebell.

What Type of Kettlebell Should You Choose?

There are different types of kettlebells available in the market. You should select a kettlebell that suits your needs and your body structure. There are certain attributes that should be kept in mind in order to select a good quality kettlebell.

Smooth Curved Handle

Quality kettlebells come with a smooth, curved handle that can be grasped anywhere. Do not select a kettlebell that has an angular or squarish angle. The handle should be round and wide enough to allow you to hold it with both hands side by side when doing two handed kettlebells. If you are selecting a vinyl-coated or a painted kettlebell, make sure that the paint is of good quality. Good quality paint would not chip, crack, or rust easily and the pristine look of your kettlebell will be maintained for a long time.

Thickness of the kettlebell handle is also an important consideration. Improper thickness of handle can place you in danger of dropping the kettlebell and injuring yourself. An improper thin grip is when you hold the handle and your fingers are meeting the palm. An improper thick grip is when you hold the hand and your fingers are too far apart. Ideally, your fingers should be one and a half inches from the palm when holding the kettlebell.

Handle to ball gap is important for pressing exercises. If it is too short or long, the kettlebell will not fall in the right spot during certain exercises. The ideal gap between handle and ball should be about two and a half inches.

A Flat Base

Look for a kettlebell that has a flat base so that it can rest on the floor without tilting. Rubber-coated kettlebells are also available but they can be unsuitable for certain exercises and when dropped it may bounce back and hit you. Rubber-coated kettlebells are easier on the floor and cause little damage to the floor when dropped accidently.

Stated Weight

It is important to check that there is no variation in the stated weight and actual weight of the kettlebell. Inexpensive kettlebells that are manufactured by untrustworthy companies may have a huge variation in their weights. So, it is better to stick with reputable companies only when selecting a kettlebell.

Kettlebell Assembling

There are two basic methods to make a kettlebell: One piece casting and two piece assembly. In two piece assembly, a handle is attached to the ball and as a result this kettlebell is not as strong and secure as a kettlebell made by one-piece casting method. The heavy ball of a kettlebell constructed using two piece assembly method may get separated from the handle during a swing and cause injury.

How to Know if You Have Chosen the Right Size?

It is important to test a kettlebell before purchasing it. There are three basic exercises that can help you to figure out if you have chosen the right size of kettlebell or not.

Place the kettlebell in one hand and lift it above your head. If you are able to lift your arm without arching your back and hold up the kettlebell for a few seconds then it is right for you.

Hold the kettlebell with both hands between your legs with your feet slightly wider than hip-distance apart. Bend your knees and swing the kettlebell. If you are able to straighten your legs without any pain and lift the kettlebell above shoulder's height then the kettlebell size is appropriate.

Hold the handle of kettlebell with both hands while standing with your feet hip-distance apart. Squat down and swing the kettlebell in between your legs. If you are able to straighten your legs without your back or shoulders hurting then the kettlebell size is appropriate for you.

Alternatives to a Kettlebell

Kettlebells can be pricey and hard to find. Even if you own a kettlebell, you cannot have it with you all the time such as while travelling or when you do not have access to gym. Some people use regular free weights such as dumbbells to perform kettlebell exercises but they are not as effective as a kettlebell. Working out with a dumbbell does not challenge your balance the same way as a kettlebell does because in kettlebells weight is concentrated in the middle, not on either side. A better cheap alternative to kettlebells is to use household containers to create a less pricey version of kettlebell.

You can use a plastic gallon filled with water, sand, salt, or gravel in place of a kettlebell. A one gallon container filled with water weighs around 8.5 pounds, which is not enough for many kettlebell exercises such as chest press. A two gallon container packed with sand or gravel weighs a respectable amount around 15 to 20 pounds, which is enough for a beginner or an intermediate workout.

It is important to test your container or jug for cracks or leaks before beginning your kettlebell training. Even with a screw cap little leakage can occur. You may use glue or duct tape to seal the opening or use a more durable container like a gas can.

Chapter 8: How Heavy Is The Kettlebell?

Since the weight of each kettlebell is usually not variable, you should be aware before buying the right weight for you. For newcomers, weights between 4 and 16 kilograms are recommended, with women normally opting for lighter weights up to 10 kilograms and men preferring heavier weights. Over time, your strength will increase, and you will be able to handle heavier weights, but it makes sense to start with lighter weights to minimize the risk of injury and to make the beginning easier.

Kettlebell is a fantastic device in your home. There's so much that you can do with a kettlebell that it would come to your mind if you read it all at once. Today, however, we are not here to talk about kettlebells and their general benefits. Here are the benefits of Kettlebell Swings. The swing is a very specific exercise that you can do like a woman with the kettlebell.

Let's get started and talk about all the kettlebell swing benefits!

The kettlebell is probably the simplest exercise machine you could have, but also one of the most versatile and useful. It's a big cast iron ball with a single handle on the top. Kettlebells does have many uses, with one of the best applications being the Kettlebell Swing.

What Is A Kettlebell Swing?

A kettlebell swing is a special exercise that you can do with the kettlebell. They begin with your legs and feet spread apart a little more than shoulder-width apart. Hold the kettlebell handle with the kettlebell between your legs, which means that you need to bend slightly over the knees.

Then start lifting the kettlebell up and out using your legs, core, and arms to generate the force needed to reach the kettlebell. The final position will have your arms outstretched in front of you and slightly above your head, holding the kettlebell, with your straight legs. Then, once you've done that, just lower it again and go through the same process that you went through to lift it in the first place.

Benefit 1: Get A Total Body Workout - Build Muscle

One of the biggest benefits of kettlebell turns is that they provide you with a total body workout that trains almost every single muscle of your body from top to bottom. The kettlebell swing is a very efficient exercise that you can do with the kettlebell.

Just to make things clear, the first stage of the swing, in which you begin to swing it upwards, requires your legs, glutes, hips, and lower back to produce the power needed to hold the kettlebell to raise. Then, once the swing is in progress and you are about to lift it, your abdomen and abdominal muscles will contract to maintain the strength and train your core. Then, when you reach the upright position of the swing, your arms, shoulders, wings, lats, and chest engage in bringing them into the position where they are above your head.

On the way down, everything happens the other way round. As you can see, a kettlebell swing is amazing for training every single muscle in your body. The result of all this, of course, is that you will end up with stronger muscles after a short while.

Of course, we all want stronger muscles, because they increase physical performance in sports, make everyday life easier, and look good. The Kettlebell Swing is a great way to get your body ready for the beach season.

Advantage 2: Kettlebell Swings Are Very Versatile

Another thing that makes the kettlebell swing such a great exercise is because it is extremely versatile, or in other words, anyone can do the kettlebell swing. This exercise, and the kettlebell, in general, is not meant for men only.

Everyone, man and woman, young and old, can swing the kettlebell. This is because a kettlebell comes in many different weights. Smaller women, older people, and younger children can start with a kettlebell weighing only 2.5, 5, 7.5, or 10 pounds, while middle-aged men or strong people generally have a 15, 20, 25, 30, or 35 Pound kettlebell with ease.

These things can range in weight from 1.5 to as much as 100 pounds and more, which means that literally, anyone can find a good kettlebell suitable for the kettlebell swing. Also, you do not have to be in the gym to make kettlebell turns.

As long as you have enough space, you can make the Kettlebell Swing at home, in the garden, in the gym, in the park or even in your office at work. There is also the fact that buying a kettlebell is much cheaper than buying various other pieces of exercise equipment.

Advantage 3: You Can Target Certain Muscles - Different Arms

Another thing we like about the kettlebell is that you can pretty much target different muscles in your body. For example, if you want a nice, even muscle workout, as we've described to advantage number one, just use both hands for the Kettlebell Swing to evenly aim at both sides of your body.

However, if you have to exercise one side of your body more than the other for any reason, you can always make a hand kettlebell swing, in which case they will aim at the side of the body that you use to make the turns especially this particular arm.

You can even increase the challenge by taking turns kettlebell swings, with one arm on one arm and the other arm on the next, literally throwing the kettlebell from one hand to the other with each side change. It's really handy to have an exercise like the Kettlebell Swing that you can choose which parts or side of your body are the most targeted.

Advantage 4: The Swing Contains More Than One Type Of Exercise

The next big benefit that is especially worth mentioning in kettlebell turns is that you can train multiple fitness aspects at the same time. A heavy kettlebell needs a lot of power to swing up and down again and again, so it's a type of weight or weight training without a doubt.

However, the kettlebell swing also involves a constant intense movement, because, with a real kettlebell swing, you never stop moving. This is a cardiovascular aspect, and if you swing over and over again, you will also train your cardiovascular system.

If you want a good exercise that allows you to train your strength and endurance, then the kettlebell swing is the way to go. It's a great exercise to work on cross-training days, where you either want to take a break from pure strength training or pure cardio training. The kettlebell swing is the best of both worlds!

Advantage 5: Cardiovascular Training with The Kettlebell

As already mentioned, the Kettlebell Swing is a kind of cardiovascular workout, which means that it trains the heart as well as the muscles. If you do not believe this, just make 20 kettlebell swings with each arm, and then 20 with both arms, and tell us your heart is not pumping so hard that you think it will explode.

This is an exercise that will pump your heart well beyond your average heart rate, which is a good thing. Cardiovascular exercise is essential to your health and well-being.

Having a healthy heart reduces the risk of having a heart attack or stroke, lowers heart rate, lowers blood pressure, helps lower cholesterol levels, and does not make your heart work so hard and for as long can continue ticking. A stronger, healthier, and the more efficient heart does not hurt in terms of physical performance either.

Advantage 6: Healthier Lungs

The next benefit of kettlebell turns is that they can help make your lungs stronger, healthier, and more efficient. Just like Kettlebell Swings, you train all your muscles and your heart, so they train your lungs.

This is a very energy-intensive form of exercise, one that needs a lot of oxygen to keep going, one that puts a lot of strain on your lungs. The faster and harder you run the Kettlebell Swings, the more your lungs need to work to provide your body with the necessary oxygen to keep going, or in other words, train your lungs to be more efficient. This type of exercise will allow your lungs to absorb and process more oxygen over time. It also makes it easier for your lungs to send oxygen to your muscles.

The overall result is that your muscles have more oxygen available to work with an increase in how long and hard they can work. There is also the fact that you will feel less or not at all when you go up the stairs or walk, not to mention that healthy and efficient lungs are less prone to breathing-related diseases.

Kettlebell Training For Women Basic Exercise

Benefit 7: Diabetes Control

Another benefit that comes with kettlebell turns is that they can help a long way in controlling your diabetes. Diabetes has to do with the inability of your body to process sugar, especially glucose, which then stays in your body and damages your liver, kidneys, and other organs. In the long run, that can be deadly.

However, the kettlebell swing can help control this by consuming unused glucose. Your muscles will burn through this glucose as you perform kettlebell swings, reducing the need for your diabetic body to process it, something it cannot do on its own.

Advantage 8: Kettlebell Training Increased Stamina For Women

Some of the benefits we have already mentioned contribute to this benefit of stamina. Kettlebell Swings help you build up your physical stamina, and that's because of other benefits that come with them, such as increased muscle strength, cardiovascular workouts, and increased lung efficiency.

In the beginning, with the obvious, stronger muscles can do more. The stronger your muscles are from kettlebell turns, the more physical power you can muster. You can lift more, jump harder, jump higher and run faster, all thanks to these kettlebell swinging muscles.

Also, your muscles need oxygen to function, and this is where your strong heart and efficient lungs come into play. Efficient lungs that are trained by kettlebell swings can absorb, process, and transmit more oxygen in the body. Your muscles need this oxygen to keep them from getting tired, and they also help stop the build-up of lactic acid, which makes your muscles burn.

After all, the strong heart that the Kettlebell Swing gives you is necessary to pump the oxygenated blood into your muscles. As you can see, all three of these things are stronger muscles, a stronger heart, and stronger lungs, all the benefits of kettlebell swings, all of which increase your ability to perform intense physical exercise over time,

Benefit 9: Increase Your Ability To Balance

Another benefit of kettlebell turns is that they can help you improve your balance. When you do the kettlebell swing, you move it between your legs while you're bent to hold it above and in front of your head, with your arms outstretched up and out.

This fast and constant shifting of positions means that your body has to compensate for these positional changes, move automatically to absorb the positional shift, and so your balance will be trained. Your proprioceptors are the receptors in your muscles that take into account position changes, and they are the things that automatically force your body to adapt to stay upright.

Just as you train your muscles or your memory, the more you do things that compel you to balance, the better your balance becomes over time. Of course, a good balance is crucial for many different aspects of life. By the way, Kettlebell Swings also help to improve your posture by strengthening your core and back muscles. A stronger core leads to a better posture and ultimately helps to keep the balance better.

Benefit 10: Weight Loss Goals

Another advantage of Kettlebell Swings is that they can help you lose a lot of weight. Simply put, your body needs the energy to function, and that energy comes from the calories you eat, or when there is a shortage of calories in your body, from your fat stores. Well, the kettlebell swing can burn up to 20 calories per minute, that's 600 calories in 30 minutes or 1,200 calories in an hour.

You might not want to do pure swings for 60 minutes, but if you do, you'll get massive calorie-burning benefits. And if you do not have enough calories in your system, your body will burn body fat to get the energy it needs and get rid of those unsightly pounds on your body.

The Kettlebell Swing also helps to increase your metabolic rate and your EPOC. The result is that your body burns a lot more calories long after you finish training than it normally would. Ultimately, the Kettlebell is a fantastic weight-loss tool. By the way, muscles burn fat, so the more muscle you accumulate kettlebell swings, the more fat you burn, yet another big advantage.

Advantage No. 11: Reduction Of Back Pain

The swinging motion of the kettlebell turns combined with the weight of the kettlebell itself can help to reduce back pain caused by tight muscles and dorsal loading of the discs. In short, this exercise can help you stretch your back, relax him, and make him well again.

The kettlebell swing is a fantastic exercise that comes with many different benefits. Your whole body from top to bottom will benefit from this exercise. The benefits of Kettlebell Swings will undoubtedly make you happier and healthier!

Women are strong and should lift heavier weights. One of the biggest misconceptions is that women should use small 3 pound weights to avoid mass formation. As mentioned earlier, women have very little growth hormone, so replenishment is not a problem.

When doing kettlebell exercises properly, you use your whole body, you ride your hips and legs, you burn a lot of calories, and you use 100s of muscle at the same time. You need to lift heavier weights to activate all of these muscles.

Here are the kettlebell weights female can use:

• 8kg / 15lbs - take-off weight

• 12kg / 25lbs - Athletic women will achieve this weight within 6 weeks, especially for two-handed swings

• 16kg / 35lbs - Stronger women will use this weight for many two-handed exercises within 6 months

7 Best Kettlebell Exercises For Women

Below are listed the kettlebell exercises that will benefit women most. It's in order of importance, so start-up and works your way down.

• KETTLEBELL SINGLE-ARM DEADLIFT

Muscles used: buttocks, thighs, quads, hips, core, back

Why it matters: The one exercise that all women should focus on. The deadlift with one arm sends the focus directly to the back of your body and into the glutes. For a strong, raised, and breathtaking back, this is the work to do.

One-arm deadlifting will also increase your heart rate and burn a lot of calories for you. Do not be afraid to increase the weight here once you master the technique.

- KETTLEBELL SINGLE LEG DEADLIFT

Muscles used: glutes, thighs, hips, core (front and back)

Why it matters: The body connects the legs and hips with the shoulders and arms across the trunk muscles. One-leg deadlift works hard in the trunk muscles connecting the shoulder to the opposite hip via the cross-body loop system.

Mastering the one-leg deadlift will not only give you a stunning torso but also protect your spine from future training injuries, and it's a great exercise for conditioning the hips, buttocks, and hamstrings!

- KETTLEBELL SWING

Muscles used: Glutes, Thighs, Hips, Quads, Core, Back

Why it matters: Once you've mastered the two exercises above, the fun begins. Kettlebell Swings will quickly become your number one fat-burning exercise.

Kettlebell Swings not only beat over 600 muscles in the body; they are also very cardiovascular. Get ready for cardio, strength, and super fun exercise in one.

- KETTLEBELL TURKISH GETTING UP

Muscles used: buttocks, thighs, hips, quads, core, triceps

Why it matters: The Turkish Get Up is a great full-body exercise that not only penetrates deep into the core muscles but also improves the mobility of the joints. If you ever feel stiff or firm, then getting up will certainly help.

The GetUp is a beautiful movement that can be enjoyed and enjoyed from start to finish. Invest time in the get-up, and your body will thank you.

- KETTLEBELL SERIES

Muscles used: buttocks, thighs, hips, quads, core, shoulders, back, biceps

Why it matters: The series is a crucial exercise that focuses on both the back and the back of the shoulders. The execution of the series, as shown below, also works in the legs and the core.

The Row exercise helps you to withdraw your shoulders and improve the look of the chest. It's also great to counteract all the sitting that so many of us have to do every day.

- KETTLEBELL SQUAT AND PRESS (BOW THRUSTER)

Muscles used: buttocks, thighs, hips, quads, core, triceps

Why it matters: There are not many muscles left unaffected by Squat and Press. You can either perform the exercise with one hand and switch after a certain number of repetitions or use two hands.

One of the biggest mistakes of this exercise is not deep enough to squat. Work hard to bring your thighs to the floor for an additional glute activation bonus.

- KETTLEBELL LATERAL LUNGE

Muscles used: buttocks, thighs, hips, quads, core

Why it matters: The lateral failure opens not only your hips but also large legs and a raised back. The deeper you can do the side tilt, the better, but you should start steadily and work to get deeper and deeper into the movement with each repetition.

- BONUS: PUSH-UPS

Muscles Used: Buttocks, Core, Chest, Triceps

Why it matters: Men have a naturally stronger torso than women, which usually results in avoidance of the push-up. If you want to strengthen your chest, core, and back of the arms, then Push-Ups are very important.

If you are struggling with full pushups, raise the height of your hands to a table. Once you can do 10 repetitions, lower your hands to a bench and finally to the floor.

Chapter 9: Back Legs And Glutes

This chapter will take a look at the different exercises that concentrate on the lower body and the back, and the different benefits one can gain from doing these exercises with kettlebells. There are very many exercises that focus on the legs and back when it comes to kettlebell training, but many of those get overshadowed by the fact that some also greatly influence other muscle groups, particularly the core muscles and the arms.

In some of these exercises, the only reason why these other muscle groups are affected is because (especially with the arms) they are the areas that initially support the weight, or the weight shifts to them momentarily during the workout. Let us begin with one such workout.

1. The Kettlebell Clean

Target muscle group: Legs, Glutes, and Back

Walkthrough: This is an exercise that can be done by itself, but is also a very important transitional move to learn. It is one of the many classic girevoy style moves, and when used in transition, is a perfect way of instigating exercises that will give you a full body workout. Though it has been used with a barbell in traditional body building for decades, the unique nature of the kettlebell clean has meant that more professional body builders are using this particular exercise to help supplement their own bar training sessions. The benefits of doing the kettlebell clean are more efficient and explosive technique that is relatively easy to learn and yields some impressive results.

To perform a kettlebell clean, first, place the kettlebell between your feet. Swing the weight upwards by shrugging your shoulders, and pulling your body and the bell up to shoulder height as you do this. The bell should end resting on your forearm, tucked into the body with your fist at your chest in what is called the 'rack' position. Bring the weight back down to between your feet to complete one rep.

As mentioned earlier, this is a vital move to learn, not only for transitional purposes but also because it can really help to build your legs and lower back.

2. The Kettlebell Goblet Squat

This is probably one of the most useful lower body exercises you can do with a kettlebell, and definitely one of the most practised exercises there is. Very similar to the conventional squat, this particular drill has a few subtle changes that make this an exercise unique to the kettlebell.

Target muscle group: Legs, glutes and back

Walkthrough: As this is a modified squat, the first position to start in would be with you standing straight, feet shoulder width apart, and hold the kettlebell in front of you close to your chest. Squat down by pushing your hips back while driving your heels into the ground, until your thighs are at a 90 degree angle or more with the ground. Return to the original standing position to complete one rep.

Remember that as with conventional squats, there is a serious danger of injury to your lower back and spine if this exercise is not done in the proper manner and with the proper posture. With that in mind, make sure that during this exercise, your back remains straight. This will not only help avoid injury, but will also help to build core strength and stability.

3. Lateral Lunge Passes

Target muscle group: **Legs, Back, Glutes**

Walkthrough: Lateral lunges are some of the less common exercises out there, though they are also somewhat important to the lower body workout, as they work slightly different groups of muscles in the lower body than traditional lunges. This interesting alternative to the traditional lateral lunge is definitely something that will add variety to an otherwise standard workout. This is more of a crossfit exercise than a fluid style exercise, and is as easy to master as it is to learn.

To begin with, start by standing straight with your feet parted shoulder width apart. With the kettlebell in your right hand, lunge to your left, ensuring that your back is straight and your hips are pushed slightly back. As you are lunging, swing the kettlebell left in the same direction of the lunge, and pass it on to your right hand as the kettle passes the midway point. Reverse the motion, passing the kettlebell from left to right this time and count the whole process as one rep.

With these lateral lunge passes, though they target the lower body, they are also very effective in building muscle strength in the arms and shoulders, as these muscles are also engaged when swinging the kettlebell from side to side.

4. The Kettlebell Deadlift.

Target muscle group: **Legs, Glutes, Back**

Walkthrough: The traditional deadlift is usually a staple in most workout regimes, with the barbell being one of the most important pieces of equipment. This exercise has proven invaluable in helping to strengthen the lower back and when done properly. It is also a very important exercise when it comes to leg and core strength, as it not only works out the lower back but helps to mold and shape the legs and glutes.

For this drill though, forget the barbell and pick up the kettlebell, as this exercise can be performed much more easily with a kettlebell, and yield the same if not better results.

To perform the kettlebell deadlift, first place the kettlebell on the floor between your feet. Keeping your back straight, squat down low and grab the kettlebell with both hands. Keeping your arms straight and your glutes tight, dig your heels into the ground and slowly rise up into the standing position, lifting the weight with you. As with the traditional barbell deadlifts, remember to maintain the proper form as you go through the motions, as this exercise can cause back injuries if done incorrectly.

5. The Two Arm Kettlebell Row

Target muscle group: **Back**

Walkthrough: When most people think of rowing exercises, they think of a rowing machine in the gym, or actually going out to a pond or lake on a boat and rowing across an expanse of water. Others will think of rowing as something that can not only be done on the water, but can also be done in the gym with a barbell or a dumbbell and a few weights. Well, now there is another way to do this fantastic drill, and that's with a pair of kettlebells.

These weights add an interesting dynamic to the exercise, and can do more than just build up muscle strength in your upper and lower back. Apart from the benefits to your arms as well, the kettlebell row can also benefit your chest and core when done properly, making this one of the most all encompassing back exercises there is.

Begin by taking two kettlebells and placing them in front of both feet. Bend over, while bending your knees slightly and keeping your back straight. Grab both kettlebells and pull them towards your stomach, keeping your elbows close to your body as you do so. Lower the weight to complete one rep.

This fluid type exercise is ideal for building up shoulder and arm strength, and the body position it requires ensures that ample core strength and stability is also built up if done correctly.

Chapter 10: Remedies To Common Mistakes During Kettlebell Exercises

Remedy 1

Before you get your hands on any kettlebell, it is critical that you practice basic movements first. The best way to do this is by starting with a few mobility exercises just to warm the joints up. You can also start with lightweight objects like water bottles to practice kettlebell swings especially if you are a beginner. This ensures that you learn mobility without having to put yourself at risk of injury.

Remedy 2

For you to effectively and efficiently practice using the force derived from the whole body, it is critical that you consider practicing the kettlebell swings first. This will go a long way in helping you experience power being transferred from the lower parts of your body to the upper parts. Just bear in mind that your back needs to be kept flat and your glutes squeezed. Sooner or later, you will be proficient performing kettlebell workout exercises with so much zeal.

Remedy 3

The next time you perform the kettlebell swing, try to perform the movement with a slower and more controlled pace. This is very critical in stabilizing and strengthening the larger groups of muscles while lowering the risk of injuries. Therefore, it is very important for you to take control of the kettlebell while moving it downwards just as it is when moving upwards. Just like any other exercise, kettlebell swing requires you to control its movement when you bring it around the head and ensure that the shoulders are stable.

Remedy 4

For a beginner, it is advisable to start by simply setting yourself small targets. Focus your attention on completing at least ten reps before you perform higher reps. Once you can handle it, you can now add a small number of reps to your workout sessions bit by bit. It is better if you talk to your trainer about the problems you might be facing. While it is a good option to workout at home, it is important that you seek expert guidance especially if you have never used the kettlebell before.

Remedy 5

Wear flat shoes with a better grip of the floor. You could also choose to perform the exercises bare feet. When you get rid of sows, you stand a chance of strengthening your feet muscles and ligaments so that you have the freedom to move around seamlessly. Alternatively, you can choose to wear converse which has been proven to strengthen both the feet and the ankles.

Chapter 11: Workouts

I thought I would include some of the best workouts that I have done in the past or I am currently doing. Although the exact timing for these workouts aren't necessary, you may get more out of your workouts if you using a stopwatch, especially the circuit workout. These are a couple of workout that I recommend you try first, then you can start trying other ones that you come across.

Kettlebell Workout 1

This one is what I would recommend you try out first. I really like this one because it's fairly simple, but really effective and will give you a nice burn. I usually do one set of the exercise in this workout. That is usually enough for me to get a really food workout. You will be performing each exercise for a minute. Then in between each exercise you are going to take a 30 second rest.

Swing (60 seconds) – The kettlebell swing is a good exercise to begin working out because it does a great job of warming you up.

30 Second Rest

Halos (60 seconds) – This is also another great exercise to start getting a good burn in your triceps, biceps, and your shoulders.

30 Second Rest

Swing (One Arm) (60 seconds) – Performing the one arm swing is really great at isolating each arm. Exercise one arm, rest for 30 seconds, then exercise the other arm.

30 Second Rest

Snatch (60 seconds) – After you get through with these, your shoulders will be really burning, along with your traps and upper back.

30 Second Rest

Clean & Press (60 seconds) – This exercise actually combines two exercises into one.

You will being to perform a kettlebell clean, rest for a second, then go right into a kettlebell press. You will perform it with one arm, for a minute, rest for 30 seconds, then perform the exercise with your other arm.

Kettlebell Workout 2

This workout that I rely like is composed of a couple of circuits. This kettlebell workout the one I recommend if you are trying to lose some excess fat because these high intensity circuits are great for getting your heart rate up and burning fat.

A circuit is when you continuously perform each exercise one after another. So with this workout you are going to have three circuits with three exercises in each. So circuit one for example you are going to perform the kettlebell swing, then immediately go into the kettlebell clean 7 press, then immediately go into the kettlebell Turkish get up. For each exercise in this workout you are going to perform them for one minute. You will take a one minute rest after you have performed one set.

Circuit 1

Kettlebell Swing (60 seconds)

Clean & Press (60 seconds) – Perform one arm, then immediately go into the second arm WITHOUT rest.

Turkish Get Up (60 seconds)

Rest 1 minute

Circuit 2

Kettlebell Swing (60 seconds)

Bent over row (60 seconds) – Perform this exercise with one arm then immediately switch and start perform the exercise with your other arm.

Windmill (60 seconds) – Same goes for this exercise as well, perform one arm then go straight into the other arm.

Rest 1 minute

Circuit 3

Kettlebell Swing (60 seconds)

Kettlebell Snatch (60 seconds)

Turkish Get Up (60 seconds)

Workout 3

This workout is especially good for building leg muscles, abs, and your lats.

Goblet Squat (60 seconds)

Rest 30 seconds

Bent over rows (60 seconds)

Rest 30 seconds

Kettlebell Snatch (60 seconds)

Rest 30 seconds

Kettlebell Press (Squatting down) (60 seconds) – This one is going to be a little bit different than the regular shoulder press because instead of standing up, you are going to be squatting as you perform the press. Make sure you don't keep your eye off of the kettlebell as you are performing this one.

Rest 30 seconds

Kettlebell Windmill (60 seconds)

Rest 30 seconds

Kettlebell Deadlift (60 seconds) You have an option of performing the deadlift with your **kettlebell**(s) in between your legs or outside of them.

How To Create Your Own Workout Plan

The three workouts that I just outlined are the workout that I have personally used and I would recommend you try them as well. I will say though, usually combine my kettlebell workouts with workouts that involve a barbell. I usually perform kettlebell workouts at least 2-3 times a week; in between those days I usually perform a good simple barbell workout. One barbell I recommend you combine with your kettlebell workouts is the 5x5 workout on Stronglifts.com (You can find the link to the page in the resource section.)

That being said, you have so many options when it comes to kettlbell workouts that it can be overwhelming. If you don't like the workouts I recommend you can find some other good ones or you can simply make your own, according to your personal fitness goals. You can pick out some of the exercises that stand out to you and incorporate them into a weekly workout routine that fits your needs. I can only show you what has worked for me, so by all means add your own style to your kettlebell workouts.

As Bruce Lee said:

"Adapt what is useful, reject what is useless, and add what is specifically your own."

— Bruce Lee

Chapter 12: Kettlebell Ultimate Workouts For Men

Do the following exercises by applying the ladder training. Start with one repetition of each workout on your right side, shifting from one exercise to the next without stopping to have a break. And then, perform repetitions of each exercise on your right side that you can increase up to three or five repetitions. Take a break for two minutes, and then do the ladder training on the left side. If grip is not that strong to do a complete ladder just on one side, do the activity alternately. Get some rest for a minute in between repetition levels. In developing and enhancing one's grip to be quicker, perform the "farmer's walk" explained below.

Kettlebell one arm snatch

Using your right hand, get a kettlebell and stand straight with the feet apart at shoulder length. Allow the kettlebell to hang in front of you at arm's length. Do a swinging motion between your legs and then pull it frontward and up. As it goes up to the level of your heart, turn it over at the back of your forearm and hit it above your head. This kettle with a single arm snatch works out the entire body in one fluid motion.

Kettlebell windmill

Once the kettlebell is above your head, turn your feet so it points 45° past the weight. Let your arm remain straight above the head, the hips moved to the right with the left hand going down the left leg. Stop, and then go back to the starting position. This movement makes the shoulders stronger at the same time works out the core.

Kettlebell one arm front squat

Position with your right elbow at the side while the weight is positioned facing the right shoulder with palm faced inwards. Hips towards the back while you get into a squat position with the thighs extended in the same direction as the floor. Stand back up. Squats using a barbell can be straining to the wrists. When using a kettlebell, there is no stress to the wrist because it remains in the neutral position.

Kettlebell one arm shoulder press

Remain standing with the palm faced frontward and the kettlebell outside the shoulder. Push the weight above the head then lower to original position. The most movable and the least steady joint in the body is the shoulder; hence, it is highly imperative to have a good form. This means allowing the elbow to remain on the side.

Strengthen your grip

Maintaining a strong grip is beneficial since it helps to increase the weight you are able to lift and the duration to keep it raised. The gird of your grip can also facilitate the translation of your upper body's strength and power. To strengthen one's grip, it helps to do the fifteen-minute farmer's walk two times per week after completing your workout or at whatever time you are able to.

Farmer's walk

Get two kettlebells. Place one for each hand hanging at arm's length on both sides. Firmly, hold on to them. Walk as long as you possibly can until you feel tired from holding the kettlebells. If you want additional challenge, grab the end of each kettlebell or you can do the walking in your toes to make this movement more difficult and develop your calf muscles. If you notice that you can already walk for more than a minute with the kettlebells, you can add more weight to the ones you are carrying.

Conclusion

Thank you again for purchasing this book on kettlebell workouts!

I am extremely excited to pass this information along to you, and I am so happy that you now have read and can hopefully implement these strategies going forward.

I hope this book was able to help you understand how kettlebell based workouts can help in weight loss and how to apply the basic principles into actions that produce results.

The next step is to get started using this information and to hopefully live a fit, active and happy life!

Please don't be someone who just reads this information and doesn't apply it, the strategies in this book will only benefit you if you use them!

If you know of anyone else that could benefit from the information presented here please inform them of this book.

Thank you and good luck!

www.ingramcontent.com/pod-product-compliance
Lightning Source LLC
LaVergne TN
LVHW011956070526
838202LV00054B/4941